TRUTH

ISBN 978-1-70516-070-1

For all works contained herein:
Unauthorized copying, arranging, adapting, recording, internet posting, public performance,
or other distribution of the music in this publication is an infringement of copyright.
Infringers are liable under the law.

Visit Hal Leonard Online at
www.halleonard.com

World headquarters, contact:
Hal Leonard
7777 West Bluemound Road
Milwaukee, WI 53213
Email: info@halleonard.com

In Europe, contact:
Hal Leonard Europe Limited
42 Wigmore Street
Marylebone, London, W1U 2RY
Email: info@halleonardeurope.com

In Australia, contact:
Hal Leonard Australia Pty. Ltd.
4 Lentara Court
Cheltenham, Victoria, 3192 Australia
Email: info@halleonard.com.au

TRUTH

ALEXIS FFRENCH

" And as we let our light shine, we unconsciously give other people permission to do the same. As we are liberated from our own fear, our presence automatically liberates others. **"**

NELSON MANDELA

I am so pleased to present this collection of songs from my *Truth* album, featuring 'Songbird', 'Canyons', 'Golden' and many more.

In writing these pieces, as we were all locked down, I imagined what the world would look like if we all asked ourselves the question *"who am I and what is my purpose in the world?"* and what we, as a human race, could create and change together. Out of that intensely personal moment, and as a reaction to feelings I could barely fathom at the time, these songs were born – as an elegy to the audacity of hope.

Truth is proof of the power of community, positive thought and collective healing, and is a direct response to the act of reflecting on my own purpose and attempting to better live my own truth.

This collection is a destination point following *Alexis Ffrench: The Sheet Music Collection* and is the most authentic representation of who I am, and what matters most to me at this moment in time.

My hope is that by shining a light through these songs, I can radiate the truth of my own journey to provide you, the pianist, with a vessel through which to amplify the essence of your soul.

Best wishes and enjoy!

Alexis Ffrench

CANYONS

BY ALEXIS FFRENCH

Copyright © 2022 UNIVERSAL MUSIC PUBLISHING LTD.
All Rights in the U.S. and Canada Administered by UNIVERSAL - POLYGRAM INTERNATIONAL PUBLISHING, INC.
All Rights Reserved   Used by Permission

10

13

ONE LOOK

WORDS AND MUSIC BY ALEXIS FFRENCH, LEONA LEWIS, JON MAGUIRE AND TAYLOR COUSINS

Lyrical, flowing and romantic

You don't need to try, you're what __ it feels to be a-

Copyright © 2022 UNIVERSAL MUSIC PUBLISHING LTD., LEONA LEWIS PUBLISHING DESIGNEE, JON MAGUIRE PUBLISHING DESIGNEE and TAYLOR COUSINS PUBLISHING DESIGNEE
All Rights for UNIVERSAL MUSIC PUBLISHING LTD. in the U.S. and Canada Administered by UNIVERSAL - POLYGRAM INTERNATIONAL PUBLISHING, INC.
All Rights Reserved   Used by Permission

with one — look. ____

These four walls we're liv-ing in, these three words, oh, they be-gin ____ with two hearts, two hearts and one look. ____ One

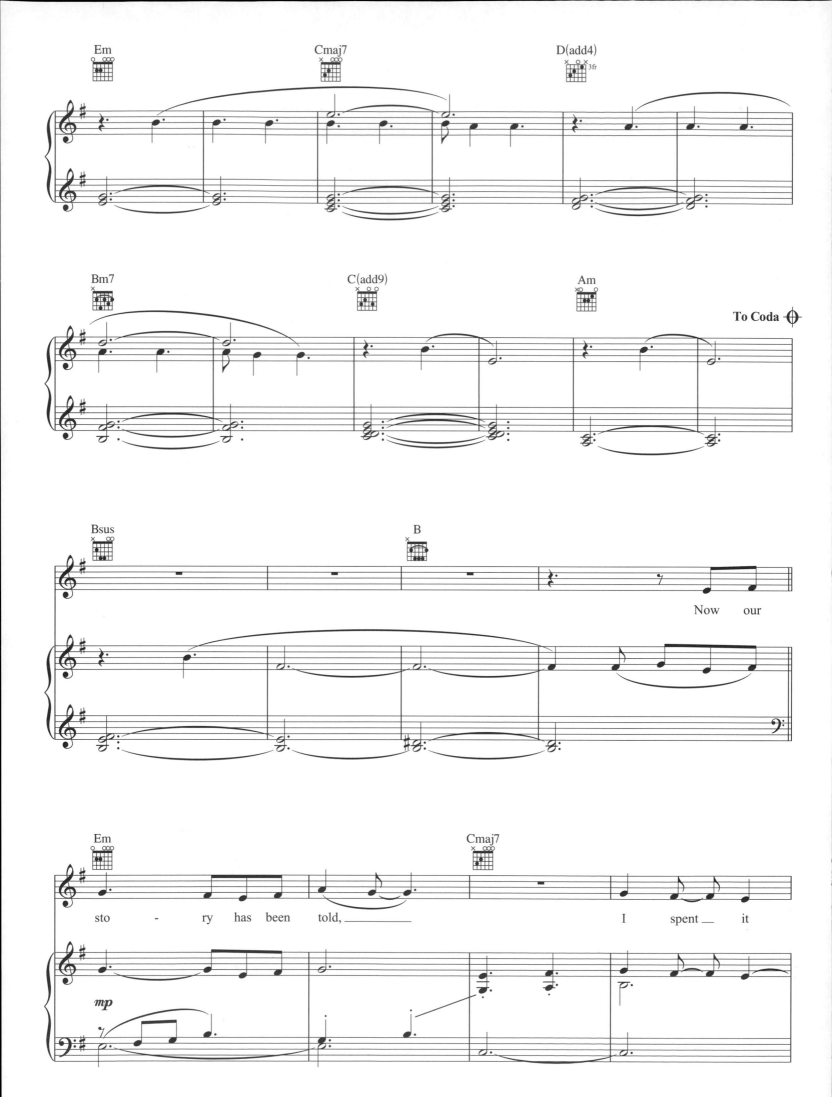

watch - ing us grow old.   I'd give ___ my

bod - y and my soul ____   for just one ___

look. ____

These   four   walls   we're   liv - ing   in,

SONGBIRD

BY ALEXIS FFRENCH

Lyrical, innocent, tender and warm

Copyright © 2022 UNIVERSAL MUSIC PUBLISHING LTD.
All Rights in the U.S. and Canada Administered by UNIVERSAL - POLYGRAM INTERNATIONAL PUBLISHING, INC.
All Rights Reserved   Used by Permission

22

HOPE, ASCENDING

BY ALEXIS FFRENCH

Copyright © 2022 UNIVERSAL MUSIC PUBLISHING LTD.
All Rights in the U.S. and Canada Administered by UNIVERSAL - POLYGRAM INTERNATIONAL PUBLISHING, INC.
All Rights Reserved   Used by Permission

GUIDING LIGHT

BY ALEXIS FFRENCH

Copyright © 2022 UNIVERSAL MUSIC PUBLISHING LTD.
All Rights in the U.S. and Canada Administered by UNIVERSAL - POLYGRAM INTERNATIONAL PUBLISHING, INC.
All Rights Reserved   Used by Permission

VIVA VIDA AMOR

BY ALEXIS FFRENCH

Copyright © 2022 UNIVERSAL MUSIC PUBLISHING LTD.
All Rights in the U.S. and Canada Administered by UNIVERSAL - POLYGRAM INTERNATIONAL PUBLISHING, INC.
All Rights Reserved   Used by Permission

40

STILL LIFE

BY ALEXIS FFRENCH

Copyright © 2022 UNIVERSAL MUSIC PUBLISHING LTD.
All Rights in the U.S. and Canada Administered by UNIVERSAL - POLYGRAM INTERNATIONAL PUBLISHING, INC.
All Rights Reserved   Used by Permission

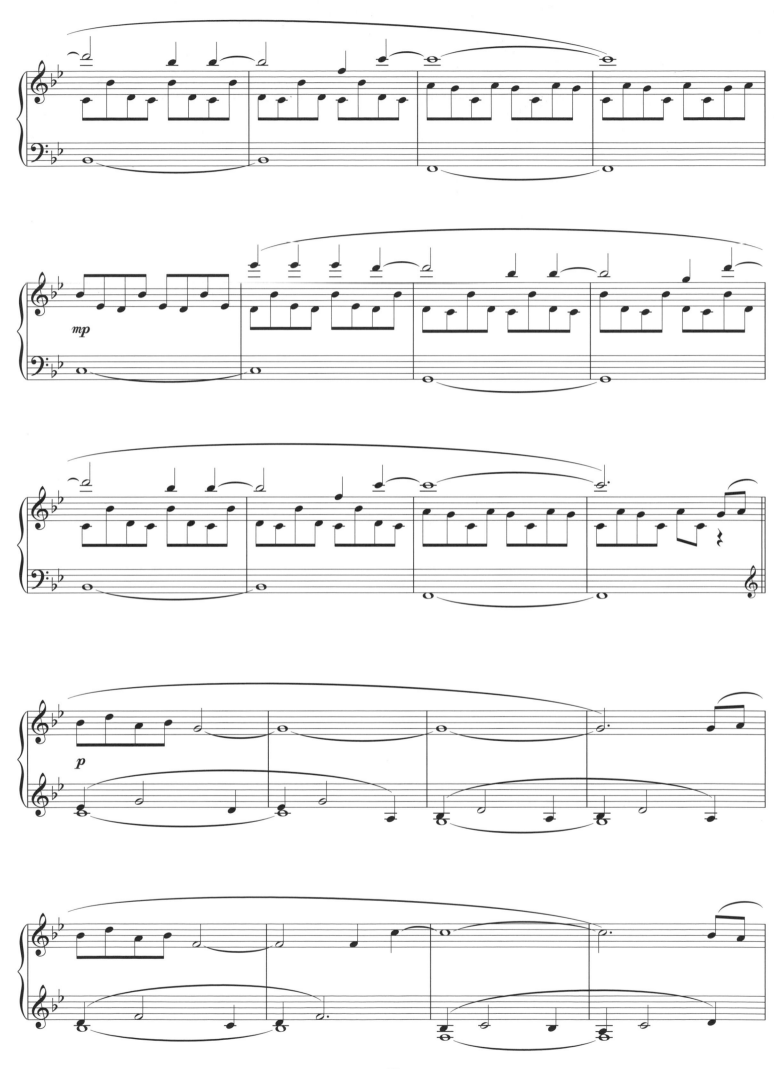

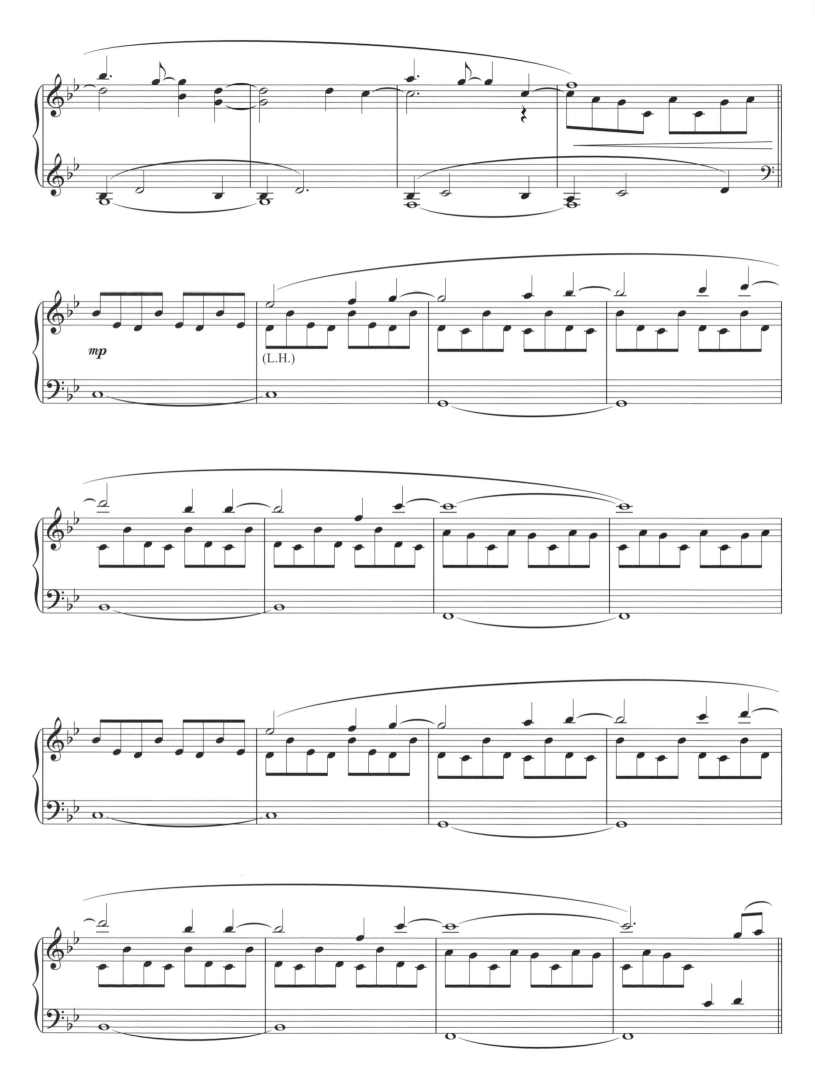

GOLDEN

BY ALEXIS FFRENCH

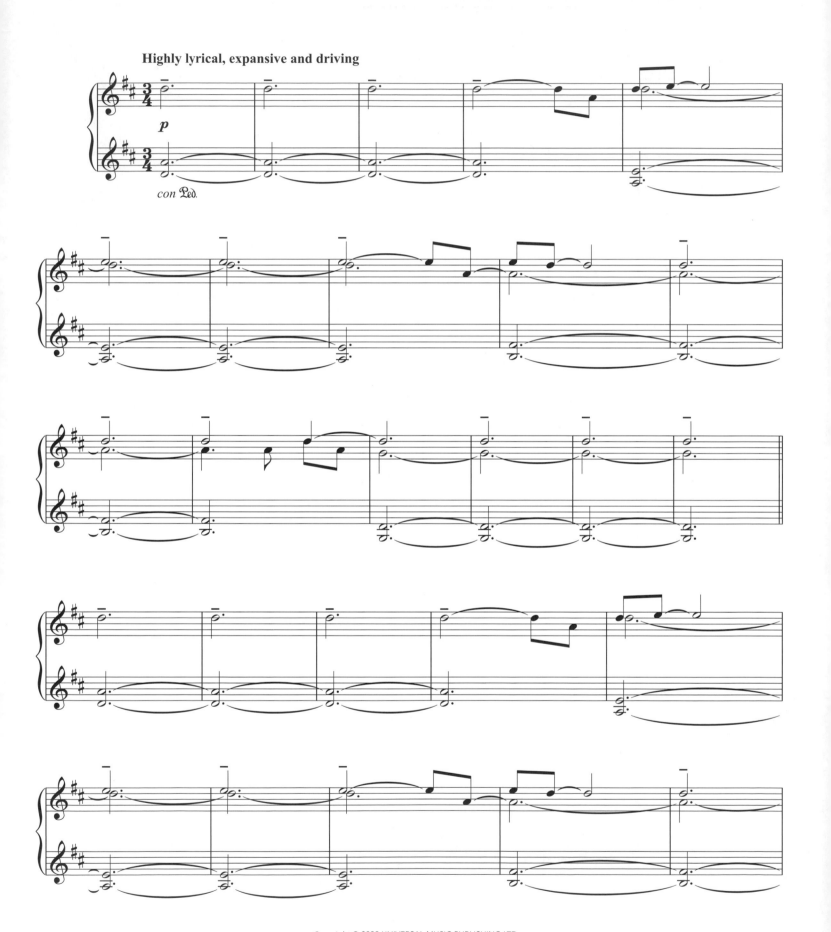

Highly lyrical, expansive and driving

Copyright © 2022 UNIVERSAL MUSIC PUBLISHING LTD.
All Rights in the U.S. and Canada Administered by UNIVERSAL - POLYGRAM INTERNATIONAL PUBLISHING, INC.
All Rights Reserved   Used by Permission

59

COLOURS

BY ALEXIS FFRENCH

Copyright © 2022 UNIVERSAL MUSIC PUBLISHING LTD.
All Rights in the U.S. and Canada Administered by UNIVERSAL - POLYGRAM INTERNATIONAL PUBLISHING, INC.
All Rights Reserved   Used by Permission

PAPILLON

BY ALEXIS FFRENCH

Copyright © 2022 UNIVERSAL MUSIC PUBLISHING LTD.
All Rights in the U.S. and Canada Administered by UNIVERSAL - POLYGRAM INTERNATIONAL PUBLISHING, INC.
All Rights Reserved   Used by Permission

A little slower

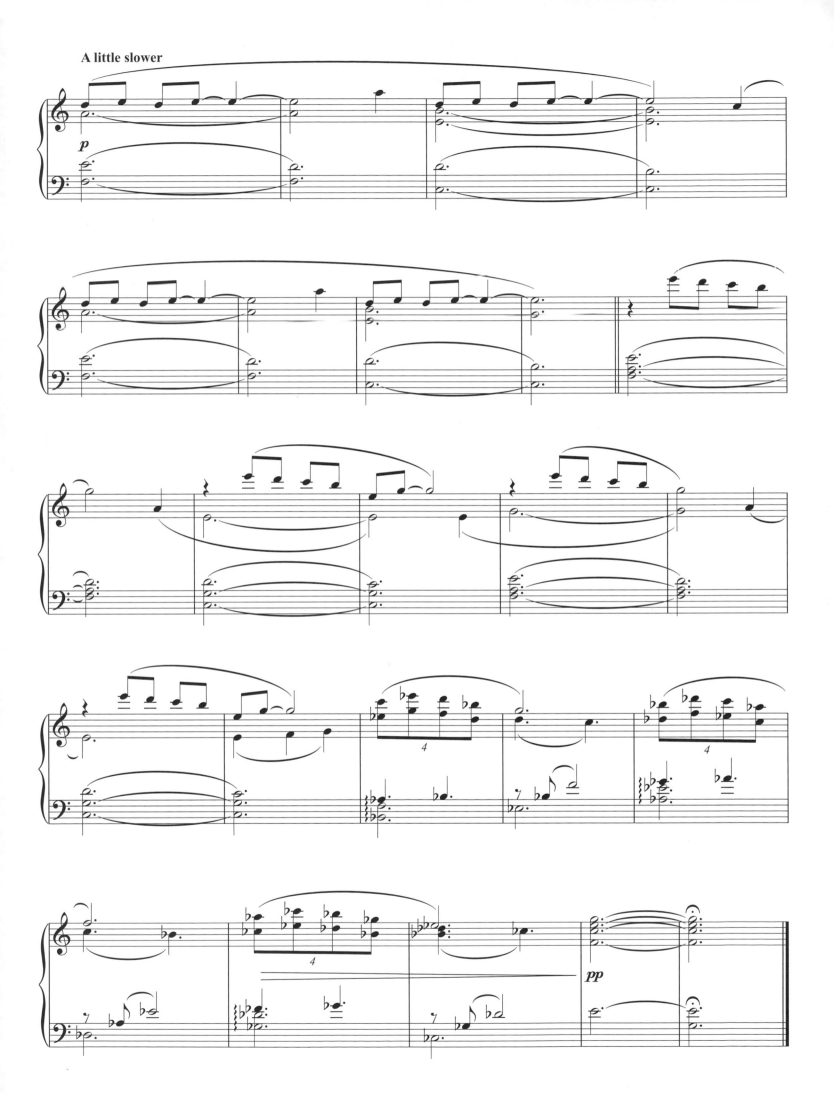

ONE LOOK
(REPRISE)

BY ALEXIS FFRENCH

Copyright © 2022 UNIVERSAL MUSIC PUBLISHING LTD.
All Rights in the U.S. and Canada Administered by UNIVERSAL - POLYGRAM INTERNATIONAL PUBLISHING, INC.
All Rights Reserved   Used by Permission

74

EVERMORE

BY ALEXIS FFRENCH

Copyright © 2022 UNIVERSAL MUSIC PUBLISHING LTD.
All Rights in the U.S. and Canada Administered by UNIVERSAL - POLYGRAM INTERNATIONAL PUBLISHING, INC.
All Rights Reserved   Used by Permission

BROKEN SUNSETS

BY ALEXIS FFRENCH

Copyright © 2022 UNIVERSAL MUSIC PUBLISHING LTD.
All Rights in the U.S. and Canada Administered by UNIVERSAL - POLYGRAM INTERNATIONAL PUBLISHING, INC.
All Rights Reserved   Used by Permission

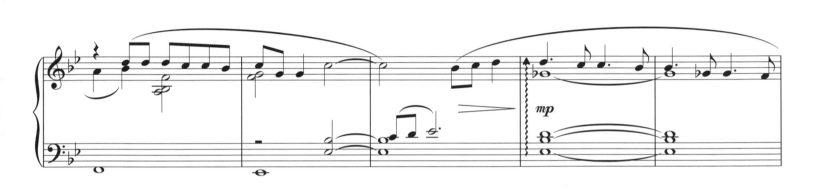